MW01196740

DISCARD

Capstone Short Biographies

African-American Inventors II

Bill Becoat, George Carruthers,
Meredith Gourdine, Jesse Hoagland, Wanda Sigur

by **Susan K. Henderson**

Content Consultant:
Robert L. Mason, Ph.D.
Teacher, Administrator, and Phenomenologist
Formerly with Chicago Public Schools

C A P S T O N E
H I G H / L O W B O O K S
an imprint of Capstone Press

C A P S T O N E   P R E S S
818 North Willow Street • Mankato, MN 56001
http://www.capstone-press.com

Copyright © 1998 by Capstone Press. All rights reserved. No part of this book may be reproduced without written permission from the publisher. The publisher takes no responsibility for the use of any of the materials or methods described in this book, nor for the products thereof.
Printed in the United States of America.

Library of Congress Cataloging-in-Publication Data
Amram, Fred M.B.
    African-American inventors / Fred M.B. Amram
    p. cm.
    Includes bibliographical references and index.
    Summary: Brief biographical profiles of five African-American inventors.
    ISBN 1-56065-361-2
        1. Afro-American inventors--Biography--Juvenile literature.
[1. Inventors. 2. Afro-Americans--Biography.] I. Title.
T39.A55 1996
609.2'273--dc20

                                       95-47863
                                          CIP
                                      AC r96

Henderson, Susan K. *African-American Inventors II.* ISBN 1-56065-697-2

Editorial credits:
Editor, Rebecca Glaser; cover design and illustrations, James Franklin; photo research, Michelle L. Norstad

Photo credits:
AP/Wide World Photos, 25, 26
Archive Photos, 4
Bill Becoat, cover, 8, 10, 14
Jesse Hoagland, 30, 32, 35
Deuce Innovator, 13
Stephen Legendre, 6, 36, 39, 42
Naval Research Laboratory, 16, 19, 21
Bob Schatz, 26

Table of Contents

Chapter 1

What Inventors Do

George Washington Carver was a famous African-American inventor. He invented more than 100 uses for peanuts. Carver was creative. Ink, medicine, and glue were some of the things he made from peanuts.

Inventors try to solve problems. They ask questions and imagine new ways of doing things. Like Carver, inventors are creative.

There are many kinds of inventors. Some inventors are scientists who work in labs. Others work at home. Some inventors work alone. Others work as part of a team.

Inventions take many shapes and forms. Some are scientific. Some are simple

George Washington Carver was a famous African-American Inventor.

Some inventors work in teams.

inventions made at home. Some are games that help people have fun. Others serve serious purposes. An invention is not always an object. A new process can be an invention. A process is a way of doing things.

Patents

A patent is an official paper. It gives inventors the right to make and sell their inventions. It prevents others from copying the invention for 17 years. Inventors apply for patents from the United States Patent and Trademark Office (USPTO). They can receive patents for a process, a plan, or a machine.

Inventors must do patent searches. A patent search means checking for patents on similar products or processes. Inventors apply for patents if no one else has invented the same thing. They must submit an application and pay fees to the USPTO.

Sometimes inventors hire patent attorneys. A patent attorney is a person who is trained in patent laws. Patent attorneys help inventors apply for patents. They may do patent searches. They make sure that legal forms are filled out correctly.

The USPTO must review the patent. A patent examiner there checks to see if the invention is new and useful. New means that the invention must be different from other inventions. In patent law, useful means that the invention must work for its intended purpose.

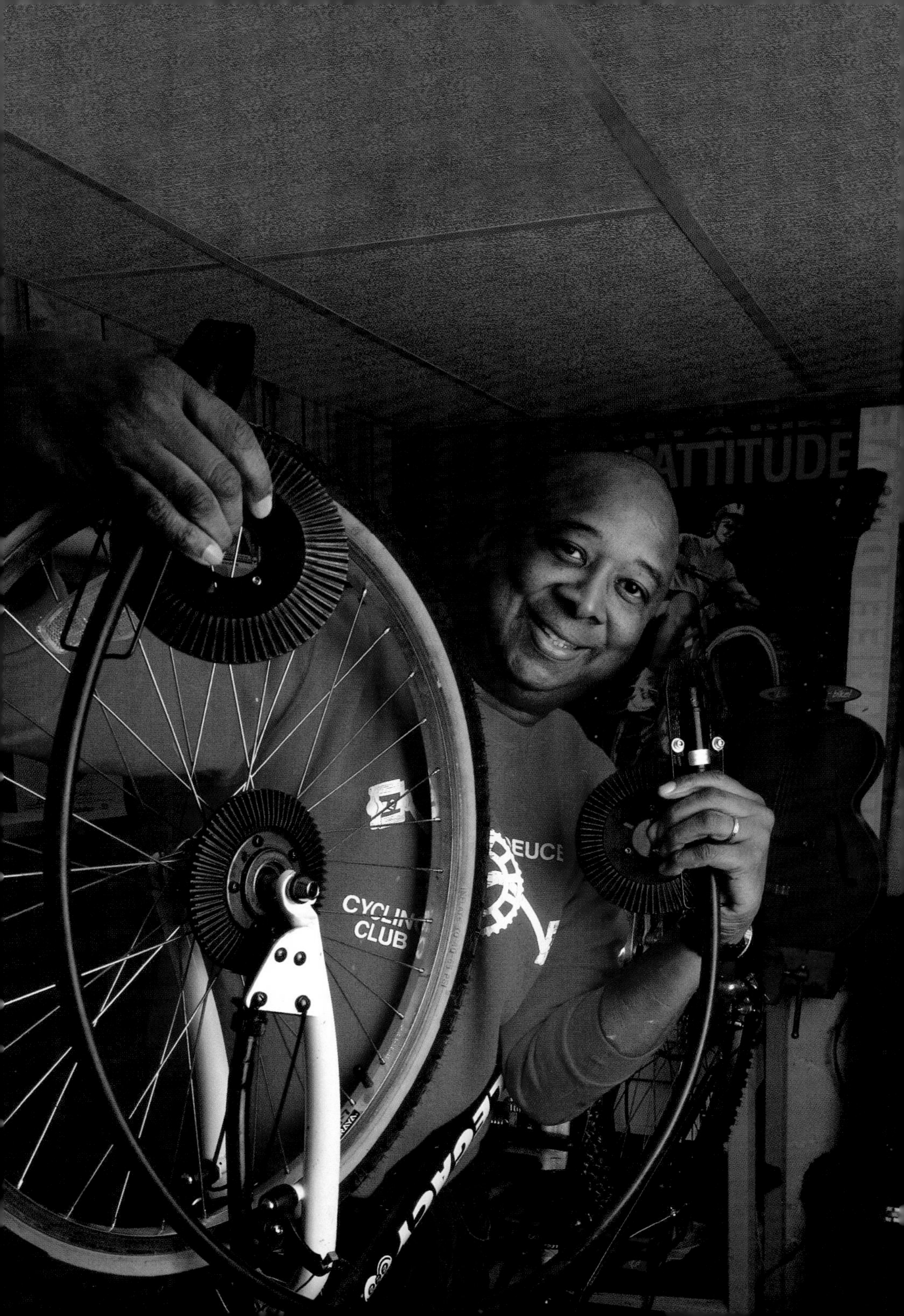
ATTITUDE
CLUB

Chapter 2

Bill Becoat

1938–

Bill Becoat was born May 25, 1938, in Centralia, Illinois. He studied cell biology in college. Biology is the scientific study of living things. A cell is a microscopic part of an animal or plant.

Becoat also learned important things outside of school. He became a mechanic as an apprentice at McDonnell Aircraft. An apprentice is someone who learns by working with a skilled person.

Becoat taught himself to play the guitar. He earned money as a folk and blues singer for three years. Becoat learned the skills needed to run a home improvement business, too. He

Bill Becoat invented the two-wheel-drive bicycle.

Both wheels are connected to the pedals on a two-wheel-drive bike.

owned and operated a home improvement company for more than 20 years.

Now Becoat works in research and development. Research and development is another name for inventing. Becoat plans to work in research and development for the rest of his life.

A New Kind of Bicycle

In 1986, Becoat was fixing his son's 10-speed bike. The chain was not working. Becoat often had to repair the chain on his son's bike. He wondered if there was a better way to make a bicycle. He imagined a two-wheel-drive bike. Two-wheel-drive means that two wheels are connected to the pedals.

Regular bikes are rear-wheel-drive bikes. Only the rear wheel is connected directly to the power source. The rear wheel and pedals are connected by a chain. The front wheel is pushed along by the rear tire.

Becoat added a flexible cable to a regular bike to make it a two-wheel-drive bicycle. Flexible means able to bend. The flexible cable connects the pedals to the front wheel. A chain connects the pedals to the rear wheel. The power goes to both wheels. Both wheels push the bike forward.

The First Two-Wheel-Drive Bike

Becoat built his first two-wheel-drive bicycle in 1987. His two-wheel-drive bike looks much like a regular bike. But its cable connects the pedals to an extra gear on the front wheel. It also has an extra gear on the rear wheel.

Becoat started with a regular bike. He had to find a way to connect the pedals to the front wheel. It could not affect the bike's steering.

Becoat had used a drill with a flexible handle at McDonnell Aircraft. The drill handle could bend in different directions. Becoat thought he could use a similar cable on the bike. The cable would carry power from the pedals to the front wheel. It would not affect the steering of the bike because it was flexible. Becoat tried the idea. It worked.

Advantages of Becoat's Bike

Becoat says the two-wheel-drive bike gives the rider better control. His bike has better traction on slippery surfaces. Traction is the force that keeps a moving object from slipping on a surface. Becoat's bike moves through slush and snow better than a rear-wheel-drive bike. The rider can handle it more easily on rough ground and on hills.

The two-wheel-drive bike gives the rider better control.

Becoat also invented a front-wheel-drive scootabike.

Becoat's two-wheel-drive bike also makes sharp turns more safely than regular bikes. The front wheel does not slide on sharp turns. Regular bikes sometimes slip and crash during sharp turns.

The chain on a two-wheel-drive bike lasts longer than a chain on a regular bike. It does not wear out as fast because the pedals are connected to both wheels.

Improving the Two-Wheel-Drive Bike

Becoat has continued to improve his bike. He owns four patents related to the two-wheel-drive bicycle. In 1993, Becoat created a conversion kit. The conversion kit is a set of parts that a person can add to a regular bike. Adding these parts will make it a two-wheel-drive bike. A person can use this conversion kit on any mountain bike.

Becoat also invented a front-wheel-drive scootabike. Front-wheel-drive means that the pedals are connected to the front wheels. This scootabike is a combination scooter and bicycle. A person can ride it like a regular bike. Or a person can stand with one foot on the scooter and push with the other foot. The scootabike can go faster than a scooter because it has a larger front wheel.

Becoat's inventions are not on the market today. But he believes they soon will be. In 1997, Becoat sold a license to make his bike and conversion kit to Rimball Enterprises, Inc. Rimball Enterprises will manufacture and sell Becoat's products. Someday many people may be riding two-wheel-drive bicycles.

Chapter 3

George Carruthers

1939–

George Carruthers was born October 1, 1939, in Cincinnati, Ohio. Carruthers was interested in science and space as a boy. He built his first telescope when he was nine years old. He read about science and astronomy. Astronomy is the study of stars, planets, and space.

Carruthers studied physics and aerospace engineering in college. Physics is the study of matter and energy. It includes the study of light, heat, sound, electricity, motion, and force. Aerospace engineering is creating and building machines for air and space travel.

George Carruthers (right) invented the Far Ultraviolet Camera.

Carruthers studied at the University of Illinois. He earned his doctorate in 1964. A doctorate is the highest degree awarded by a university.

Far Ultraviolet Camera

Carruthers went to work for the Naval Research Laboratory in Washington, D.C. He worked in the Space Science Division. He invented a camera that takes pictures of things in space using ultraviolet light. Ultraviolet light comes from the sun. People cannot see it. Ultraviolet light causes suntans and sunburns.

Scientists wanted to learn more about the earth and stars. Gases like oxygen and hydrogen are important parts of the earth's atmosphere. But these gases are colorless. People cannot see them or study them. They needed a way to take pictures of the gases.

Carruthers invented a camera that could take pictures of oxygen, hydrogen, and other gases. The camera is called the Far Ultraviolet Camera. The pictures helped scientists learn which gases were in Earth's outer atmosphere.

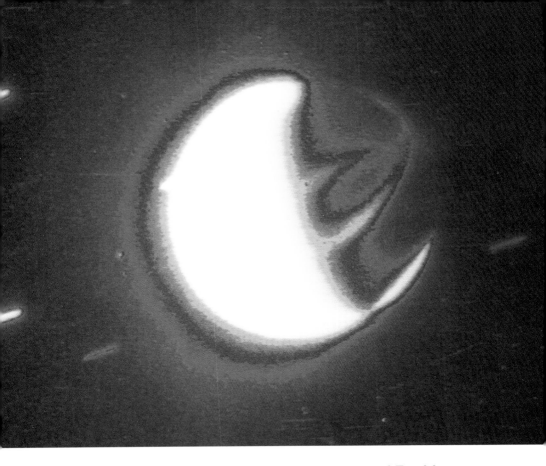

The Far Ultraviolet camera took this picture of Earth's atmosphere in ultraviolet light.

The Far Ultraviolet Camera takes pictures in ultraviolet light. The ultraviolet light pictures taken with Carruthers' camera show gases as colors. This helps scientists learn about the atmospheres of Earth and other planets.

19

Different Models, Different Uses

Scientists sent the camera to space on a short rocket flight in 1967. The camera worked. But Carruthers kept improving his camera. He made different models for different uses. Some ultraviolet cameras were used in satellites. A satellite is a spacecraft that orbits around the earth. Scientists and astronauts used later models of the camera on longer space flights.

Carruthers created a large camera that could sit on the surface of the moon. He mounted the camera on a large, sturdy tripod. A tripod is a stand with three legs. Astronauts put the Lunar Ultraviolet Camera on the moon. It was part of the Apollo 16 mission in 1972. It took pictures of the earth in ultraviolet light.

The camera also took pictures of distant stars and planets. The camera detected hydrogen deep in space. Understanding what other stars and planets are made of helps scientists understand Earth better. They learn how the earth is different from other planets.

Carruthers has adapted the ultraviolet camera for many uses. He worked on the

George Carruthers worked on the Global Imaging Monitor.

Global Imaging Monitor. This machine will observe Earth's outer atmosphere. It will orbit on an air force satellite. The Global Imaging Monitor contains two ultraviolet cameras. The cameras will take pictures as the satellite orbits Earth.

Chapter 3

Meredith Gourdine

1929–

Meredith Gourdine was born September 26, 1929, in Livingston, New Jersey. He grew up in New York City. In college, Gourdine studied several areas of science. One was electrical engineering. Electrical engineering is creating and building things that use electricity.

Since then, Gourdine has invented things that use electricity. Gourdine has received more than 70 patents. He has solved many problems with his inventions.

Gourdine was a track athlete at Cornell University in New York. An athlete is someone trained in a sport or game. During college, Gourdine earned a spot on the U.S. Olympic

Meredith Gourdine invented a new process for painting cars.

Team. This team is a group of athletes that represents the United States at the Olympic Games. The Olympic Games are sports contests between athletes from many nations.

The 1952 Olympics were held in Helsinki, Finland. Gourdine won a silver medal for the broad jump. A silver medal is an award given to the second-best athlete at an Olympic event.

Gourdine studied at the California Institute of Technology. He conducted research and experiments while studying for his doctorate. Research is finding out about something by reading and doing experiments. Gourdine earned a doctorate in engineering science in 1960. Gourdine started his own company the same year. He named it Gourdine Laboratories.

Gourdine has invented things for many years. He has manufactured and sold his inventions. His most successful invention was a machine that painted objects on factory assembly lines. An assembly line is a group of workers and machines that puts together a product. Each

Gourdine conducted research and experiments at the California Institute of Technology.

Workers and machines paint cars on assembly lines.

worker or machine completes one step. The worker or machine then passes the product to the next person or machine.

Painting Cars and Bicycles
Cars and bicycles were sometimes poorly painted on assembly lines. Hard-to-reach corners and curved surfaces did not always get covered with paint. Later, the unpainted metal could rust and fall apart.

Gourdine invented a new method of painting for factories. His method used powdered paint and electrical charges. Gourdine invented a machine that put a positive electrical charge on the powdered paint. The machine put a negative charge on the car or bike. This caused the powdered paint to jump onto a bike or car as it passed on the assembly line.

The powdered paint stuck to the object like paper clips stick to a magnet. In the factory, paint guns sprayed the cars or bikes as they passed on a conveyor belt. The electrical charges made the powdered paint stick.

Then the machine heated the car or bike. The heat melted the powdered paint and made it look like regular paint. The paint covered all parts of the car or bike. Gourdine invented this method in the 1960s. Many factories used this painting method. Today, factories use even newer painting techniques.

The Incineraid

Many factories once used incinerators to get rid of their garbage. Incinerators are furnaces in which garbage is burned. They produce smoke and other pollution.

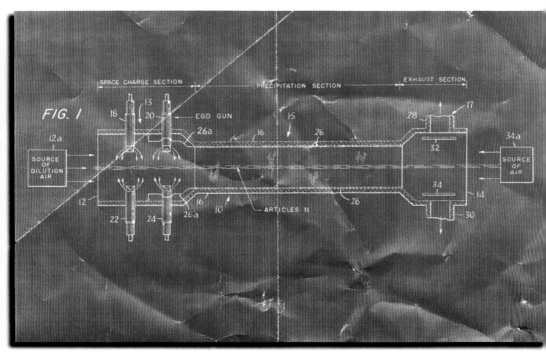

Gourdine's method of painting used electrical charges.

Gourdine invented the Incineraid in the late 1970s to help solve the pollution problem. The Incineraid reduces pollution caused by incinerator smoke. It puts electrical charges on smoke particles. Then the particles are trapped on a surface. The surfaces are easy to clean. The Incineraid can trap any type or size of particle.

Creating and selling the Incineraid was difficult. Gourdine and his team had to test and improve the idea. They had to find buyers who wanted the Incineraid. They had to raise money to build models. They built one prototype for New York City. A prototype is a model used to test an idea or product.

New York City officials decided to order 500 Incineraids. In 1980, the New York state legislature passed a law. A legislature is a group of people that makes laws. The new law said all garbage in New York must be buried. The law meant that New York City did not need Incineraids. Other big cities also stopped using incinerators. They realized incinerators caused too much pollution.

Gourdine likes inventing because he likes solving problems. He has received many patents for his inventions. His engineering background has helped him invent.

In 1991, Gourdine was elected to the National Academy of Engineering. This organization elects only a few people each year. Gourdine's election means other engineers think he is one of the best engineers in the country.

Chapter 5

Jesse Hoagland

1939–

Jesse Hoagland was born May 1, 1939, in Princeton, New Jersey. He grew up in Trenton, New Jersey.

Hoagland valued fitness. He was an athlete. Hoagland took part in basketball, swimming, and track when he was in high school. He continued playing sports after he graduated.

Hoagland enjoyed body building. Body building means lifting weights to make muscles stronger. People who lift weights use barbells. A barbell is a long metal bar with weights on each end. The bar is usually straight.

When he was older, Hoagland ran a gym where he and others could lift weights. He knew

Jesse Hoagland invented the Safety Squat Bar.

Hoagland knew that lifting weights would help him stay fit.

that lifting weights would help him stay fit. But one evening he hurt his back while doing squats. Squats help athletes strengthen their leg muscles.

Hoagland was upset. He wanted to lift weights without getting hurt. He decided to find a safer way of lifting weights.

Inventing the Safety Squat Bar

Hoagland went home from the gym. He thought about making a better barbell. He drew a picture of the first Safety Squat Bar in just 15 minutes.

After he made his first drawing, Hoagland built a prototype. The first model did not work well enough to satisfy him. Hoagland made new models. He asked athletes in his gym to try each new squat bar. Their ideas helped Hoagland improve the Safety Squat Bar. Three years later, Hoagland had a product he liked. He received a patent for the Safety Squat Bar in 1982.

How the Safety Squat Bar Works

The Safety Squat Bar is safer than other bars because of its shape. The bar has a bend at each end. The weights are put on the bent part of each barbell. This helps distribute the weight more evenly on an athlete's back and shoulders. There is a special rack that holds the Safety Squat Bar. Handles on the rack allow athletes to lift more easily.

The Safety Squat Bar has a thickly padded yoke. A yoke is a frame that goes around the shoulders and neck. The yoke helps the bar balance easily on the athlete's shoulders. Because it balances easily, it puts less pressure on an athlete's knees and back. Athletes who work with straight barbells often have knee and back problems.

The Safety Squat Bar allows athletes to keep their backs straight while doing squats. This is important for avoiding injuries to the lower back. It also lets athletes lift heavier weights during squat exercises. Lifting heavier weights helps athletes become stronger in a shorter period of time.

Manufacturing

Hoagland asked companies to manufacture his Safety Squat Bar. The companies turned him down. He decided to make the product on his own. Hoagland had once been a factory mechanic. He knew how to work with steel.

At first he made the bars at night in the factory where he worked. Then he built them in

The Safety Squat Bar has a padded yoke. The yoke rests on the athlete's shoulders.

his garage. Later he bought a factory and hired other workers.

Hoagland now sells his Safety Squat Bar to college and professional sports teams. Athletes can lift weights more safely with Hoagland's Safety Squat Bar.

Chapter 6

Wanda Sigur

1958–

Wanda Sigur was born May 26, 1958, in New Orleans. She attended Rice University in Houston, Texas.

When she was in college, Sigur studied materials science. Materials scientists experiment with elements used for building, such as steel, plastic, and aluminum alloys. An alloy is a mixture of two or more metals. Materials scientists study the strength and weight of building materials. They study how much a material will bend before it breaks.

Fixing Space Shuttle Fuel Tanks

Sigur works for a company that builds things for the National Aeronautics and Space

Wanda Sigur works to prevent cracks in the space shuttle fuel tanks.

Administration (NASA). She is the leader of the Intersection Crack Investigation Team. Sigur and her 45 team members work to prevent cracks in space shuttle fuel tanks. A space shuttle is a spacecraft that carries astronauts into space and back to Earth. Cracks often form where the metal pieces of a fuel tank join. These places are called intersections.

The outside fuel tanks of space shuttles are built from an aluminum-lithium alloy. Aluminum and lithium are lightweight metals. This alloy makes space shuttles and rockets lighter. However, it cracks easily at joints where pieces are joined together. Sigur's job is to make sure there are no cracks.

The cracks are very small and hard to see. Sigur and her team use X rays to detect the cracks. X rays can pass through solid objects. Engineers use X rays to take pictures of the insides of the metal. The pictures show if there are any cracks. Sigur and her team members invent solutions to solve this problem and other problems.

Sigur leads the Intersection Crack Investigation Team.

Space Plastic

NASA needed a material that was stronger and lighter for making space shuttle parts. If the space shuttle weighed less it could fly more easily. The old process of making space shuttle parts required engineers to heat the parts. Engineers heated them in an autoclave. An autoclave is a large oven used to apply pressure

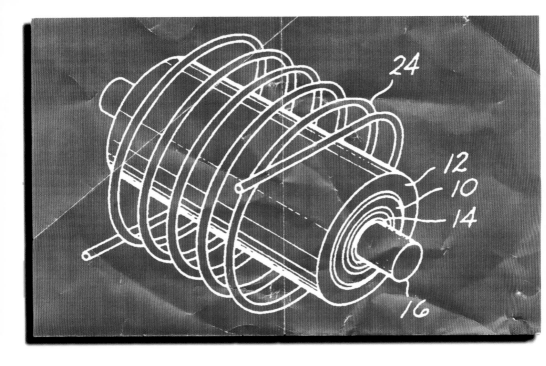

Sigur invented a plastic material that could be heated using coils.

and heat. The space shuttle fuel tank is more than 100 feet (30 meters) long. But an autoclave is only about 15 feet (.5 meters) long. So engineers had to make the tanks in sections. Each section had to be joined together. The seals had to be very tight so the tanks could hold liquid. The parts used to make the seal added extra weight.

Sigur invented a new process to make big parts of the space shuttle out of plastic. The process did not require using an autoclave. The plastic could be heated using coils. Engineers could make bigger parts that weighed less.

Sigur patented her invention in 1992, but NASA has not used the process. It was too expensive to build new facilities for making plastic. It was cheaper to improve the aluminum alloy using the equipment they already had.

NASA engineers added lithium to the alloy to make it lighter. Lithium is the lightest known metal. It is dangerous to work with. But the engineers found a way to use it safely. Adding lithium to the aluminum made the space shuttle weigh less.

Scientists and engineers often come up with new ideas that are not used. This is a normal part of inventing. Sigur does not get discouraged. She likes solving problems. She feels successful even if people do not use her inventions.

Words to Know

aerospace engineering (AIR-oh-spayss en-juh-NIHR-ing)—creating and building machines for air and space travel

alloy (AL-oi)—a mixture of two or more metals

apprentice (uh-PREN-tiss)—someone who learns by working with a skilled person

assembly line (uh-SEM-blee LINE)—a group of workers and machines that puts together a product

autoclave (AW-tuh-clave)—a large oven used to apply pressure and heat

materials science (muh-TIHR-ee-uhls SYE-uhnss)—the study of elements used for building, such as steel, plastic, and aluminum

patent (PAT-uhnt)—a legal paper that gives inventors the right to make and sell their inventions

physics (FIZ-iks)—the study of matter and energy, including light, heat, electricity, and motion

prototype (PROH-tuh-tipe)—a model used to test an idea or product

two-wheel-drive (TOO-WEEL-DRIVE)—when two wheels are connected to the power source

ultraviolet light (uhl-truh-VYE-uh-lit LITE)—light from the sun that people cannot see

yoke (YOKE)—a frame that goes around the shoulders and neck

To Learn More

Amram, Fred M. B. *African-American Inventors.* Mankato, Minn.: Capstone Press, 1996.

Hayden, Robert C. *9 African American Inventors.* Frederick, Md.: Twenty-First Century Books, 1992.

Jeffrey, Laura S. *American Inventors of the 20th Century.* Springfield, N.J.: Enslow Publishers, 1996.

McKissack, Patricia and Fredrick McKissack. *African-American Inventors.* Brookfield, Conn.: Milbrook Press, 1994.

NASA engineers improved the space shuttle fuel tank.

Useful Addresses

Black Inventions Museum, Inc.
P.O. Box 76122
Los Angeles, CA 90076

International Inventors Assistance League
345 West Cypress Street
Glendale, CA 91204

Inventors Clubs of America
P.O. Box 450261
Atlanta, GA 31145-0261

United States Patent and Trademark Office
2121 Crystal Drive
Arlington, VA 20231

Internet Sites

3M Collaborative Invention Unit
http://mustang.coled.umn.edu/inventing/
  inventing.html

African-american (BLACK) Inventors Series
http://edcen.ehhs.cmich.edu/~rlandrum/
  index1.html

Inventure Place: National Inventors Hall of Fame
http://www.invent.org

Three Dimensional Publishing's TDPNewsletter for Young Inventors
http://www.erols.com/tdpedu/yingl.htm

Young Inventors Network International Site
http://www.wirehub.nl/~invent/newyin.htm

Index